PERSONAL BOOKLET

JOURNEYS

Copyright © CWR 2008
Published 2008 by CWR, Waverley Abbey House,
Waverley Lane, Farnham, Surrey GU9 8EP, UK.
Registered Charity No. 294387. Registered Limited
Company No. 1990308. Reprinted 2009
Bible reading notes included in this booklet previously
published by CWR in the July/August 2006 issue of *Lucas
on Life Every Day*, by Jeff Lucas.
The right of Jeff Lucas to be identified as the author of
this work has been asserted by him in accordance with
the Copyright, Designs and Patents Act 1988, sections
77 and 78.
Questions for group discussion: Jeff Lucas and
Andy Peck.

For a list of our National Distributors visit
www.cwr.org.uk/distributors
Unless otherwise indicated, all Scripture references are
from the Holy Bible: New International Version (NIV),
copyright © 1973, 1978, 1984 by the International Bible
Society.
Concept development, editing, design and production
by CWR.
Printed in England by Bishop Printers.
ISBN: 978-1-85345-484-4

DAILY READINGS: **JEFF LUCAS**
GROUP DISCUSSION QUESTIONS:
JEFF LUCAS AND ANDY PECK

CWR Applying God's Word
to everyday life and relationships

CONTENTS

Introduction   3

How to Use   4

Session 1: Pressure Points   5

Session 2: Nothing but the Truth   12

Session 3: Big-Picture Thinking   19

Session 4: Moments of Truth   26

Session 5: Painful Times   33

Session 6: Risen Indeed   40

INTRODUCTION

IT WAS Gene Kelly who, in 1952, immortalised the song 'Singing in the Rain'. As he celebrated that 'glorious feeling', he created a piece of classic movie history. But beyond simply a few fancy footsteps and a catchy tune, is it really possible to sing when it's raining? When trials and troubles seem to gang up on us, or when we get mugged by another one of life's little surprises, what happens to our faith?

Have you ever had one of those weeks where everything appeared to be collapsing around you, people whom you thought you could depend upon disappeared and God wasn't in conversational mood – or so it seemed? I certainly have. Weeks like that are just part of life – they are guaranteed. But, as followers of Jesus, we can learn how to sing in the rain, quite literally, without becoming unreal about our challenges or resorting to a superficial, happy-clappy faith. Let's visit the second half of Mark's Gospel and take another long look at Jesus as He steers His way through His last seven days on earth. He was very well aware of trouble ahead, but trekked across His battlefield of blood, sweat and tears with poise, dignity and passion.

There's encouragement, inspiration and a few surprises in store. So join me on this journey – and let's learn from Jesus how to dance in a downpour.

How to use

This resource is designed to include all you will need for six small-group sessions. It comprises six DVD clips, group discussion questions based on each clip and Bible readings to be used between each session.

PREPARATION

1. Watch the DVD clip before the meeting.

2. Use the icebreaker to get people chatting. Select the questions that you think would be most useful for your group to look at. You may want to use them all, depending on the time you have available. We suggest you plan for 30–45 minutes.

THE SESSION

1. Play the DVD clip first and go straight into the icebreaker question.

2. Use the questions you have selected.

3. Move from discussion into prayer. There's a prayer included in the material which you could finish with at the end.

4. Encourage the group to use the daily readings in the days between sessions. The readings expand and build on the topics covered in the DVD. If the group members are not used to daily Bible reading, encourage them to develop this habit. If the group members are already into a routine of Bible reading and prayer each day you might want to discuss how best to work these new readings into their time.

5. You could start the next session by reviewing how the group found the daily readings. What did they learn? Do they have questions to raise? How did God speak?

Session 1:
Pressure Points

ICEBREAKER:
Is the desire to 'fix problems' generally a male trait?

FOR GROUP DISCUSSION:
- Most people have things that 'push their button'. Which things push your button? What makes you react?

- Thinking back over the last few months, when was your time of greatest pressure? What did you do (if anything) to relieve it?

- Jesus noticed small details. How does that make you feel? Do you feel cared for – or paranoid about making the wrong decision?

• Do you feel under pressure to respond quickly if someone says something negative about the Christian faith? What questions might you need to ask them, before responding?

• Were the questions Jesus asked genuine? (After all, didn't He know the answers?)

• What sort of fruit do you look for in your life or ministry?

PRAYER:
Lord,
Teach me how to respond
rather than react;
to speak and live from a place of peace
rather than in hurry and panic.
Life brings pressure:
Teach me poise.
Amen.

IN THE vintage British television show *Dad's Army*, Corporal Jones rushes around screaming at the top of his voice, 'Don't panic! Don't panic!' – while he himself is frantic agitation on legs. One of my many weaknesses is that I tend to react quickly rather than responding calmly, when the ocean of life gets choppy. My flawed logic is simple: why pray when you can flap?

Emotional turbulence seems to come to me quite naturally. And I like to fix things, *now*. While I was writing, the telephone rang and details of a situation emerged that is frustrating – and I *so* want to sort it right away – which is seldom the best idea. Pausing can restore our emotional equilibrium; there is continual encouragement towards self-control in the New Testament, especially in Peter's writings, a man who graduated from Impetuous University (1 Pet. 1:13; 5:8; 2 Pet. 1:5–7).

Jesus rode into the ancient city, a picture of poise and peace, master of an unbroken colt. He knew very well that His riding into town in this way was the action of a returning triumphant warrior (and more importantly, Messiah) that would provoke the religious leaders and would begin His walk to the cross. He also knew that most would misunderstand His actions and would look to promote Him as a political hero. But He is calm; He visits the Temple and sees all the seething corruption there – and then walks away, leaving the second epic cleansing of that place until the next day. Jesus knows well how to do pressure, holding Himself together regardless of what was going on inside.

Prayer: Lord, when I am in circumstances beyond my control, give me grace to control myself and walk in peace. Amen.

The Prince of Peace comes

BIG PICTURE:
Mark 11:1–11
1 Peter 4:7

FOCUS:
'When they brought the colt to Jesus and threw their cloaks over it, he sat on it.' (Mark 11:7)

Jesus knows

… how to do

pressure …

Temper tantrums?

FOCUS:
'Then he said to the tree, "May no-one ever eat fruit from you again." And his disciples heard him say it.' (Mark 11:14)

THE reality television show *I'm a celebrity, get me out of here* drops a handful of previously pampered famous types into a steaming jungle, where food is rare, sleep is fitful and personalities clash. Tempers often flare like the temperature, because pressure changes us, and scary Jekyll-and-Hyde-type transformations take place when stomachs rumble.

Crisis wears my patience thin. I am less willing to suffer fools gladly – or notice that it might be me that's playing the fool – when life is dark. Now, as Jesus prepares Himself for major confrontation in Jerusalem, He is most likely stressed and certainly hungry – the text tells us so.

At first glance, it looks as if Jesus is throwing a petulant strop when He finds that the fig tree is bare – especially as this was not the fruit season. This is the first and only time that Jesus used His supernatural power to destroy something. (The expulsion of the demons into the pigs which then drowned in Mark 5:13 is a possible exception, but it was unleashed demonic power that caused that event.) Was Jesus just having a bad day and an innocent tree got in the way? Or is this some Harry Potter-type magic, attention-grabbing wizardry with little purpose?

Look again: here Jesus is showing His unswerving commitment to His mission, as He exposes the withered barrenness that Israel had fallen into. Far from being a hot-headed reactionary, Jesus wants His disciples to see an enduring prophetic reminder about why He had come.

Jesus was no thoughtless prophet or volcanic hothead. Next time you're exhausted, traffic is thick, and dinner is burned, respond – don't react.

Prayer: Help me to stay on track when the path gets rough; may my character be strong enough for storms. Amen.

NO ONE relishes trouble. We all pick the quiet life rather than the din of tribulation. But there are times when we need to choose to do what is right, even though we know we'll be in hot water as a result. When Jesus bursts into the Temple courts and creates chaos as He cleanses the place, it is not the first time. John records a previous visit there, where He used a whip to drive the gaggle of extortionists from the place (John 2:13–22). Back then His action had understandably stirred up trouble; some challenged His authority for what seemed such an outrageous act (John 2:18). But now He is doing it all again, overturning the tables of the twisters, releasing sacrificial doves in a flurry of feathers and demanding that those who used the courts as little more than a short cut from the Mount of Olives show a bit more respect. Now, as then, what He did would create trouble, only this time it was worse; the religious leaders were 'looking for a way to kill him' (Mark 11:18). But He refused to back off.

The principle was worth the price and Jesus knew without question that He was in the right, as He quoted both Isaiah and Jeremiah in justification for this cleansing. The venue for this striking scene was most likely the court of the Gentiles: the only place where non-Jews could worship had been turned into a marketplace. Sometimes, to use Peter's term, we just have to learn to suffer for doing what is right.

Prayer: Gracious God, give me courage to live by Your Word, even when obedience will create trouble for me. Amen.

Do what's right, even if it costs

BIG PICTURE:
Mark 11:15–19
1 Peter 3:8–22

FOCUS:
'On reaching Jerusalem, Jesus entered the temple area and began driving out those who were buying and selling there.' (Mark 11:15)

The principle

was worth

the price …

Faith and trouble

BIG PICTURE:
Mark 11:20–26
Luke 22:31–34

FOCUS:
'I tell you the truth, if anyone says to this mountain, "Go, throw yourself into the sea," and does not doubt in his heart but believes that what he says will happen, it will be done for him.' (Mark 11:23)

I HAD a real problem with these verses in my early years as a Christian. All this talk of faith being able to move mountains and throw them into the sea made me feel more defeated than encouraged. The thought of commanding a towering peak to pop into the ocean seemed obviously quite impossible, and I wasn't blinded to the fact that such a thing had never, ever been done – even by Jesus. Back then, Adrian Plass famously wrote of his attempts to move a paper clip an inch by using prayer; but neither Everest, nor tiny office accessories were going anywhere as a result of his faith. So what is Jesus teaching us here?

The rabbis used the term 'moving mountains' to describe the ability to overcome huge obstacles and seemingly impossible difficulties (Zech. 4:7). Here Jesus calls us to navigate our way through the tough times with believing prayer; and He also commands us to clear out the clutter of doubt and bitterness too. When the clouds gather in someone's life, concentrate on praying not only for their deliverance but also for their faith. Prophesying all the difficulties and spiritual buffetings that would come to Peter's life, Jesus promised that He would pray for the headstrong fisherman 'that his faith might not fail'. Ironically, trouble is often the fertiliser that grows greater faith; so as we walk through the tough times with a determination to trust and pray, we grow in grace and find God is truly faithful.

Don't try to relocate a hill or nudge a paper clip today. But do trust.

Prayer: Lord, give me a gift of faith, especially when tempted towards unbelief. Help me to navigate with confidence in You. Amen.

I AM a blabber – ask anyone who knows me. I wear my heart on my sleeve, don't mind telling you everything that is going on and am quick to share my opinions. Put me in a time of trouble and my capacity to be Mr Motor-Mouth increases alarmingly.

But I'm slowly learning that life doesn't need to be about us telling everybody everything we know and feel. On the contrary, when our mouths are in fifth gear and our brains are in neutral, we are more likely to show people how *little* we know.

As Jesus refuses to blurt out an answer to the pressing questions of the religious, He isn't playing games – rather His silence is confronting them with the truth. Much as they wanted to, they couldn't deny the power of John the Baptist's ministry of three years earlier – it would have been politically disastrous to do so, as John was a hero to the people. In this case, silence was used with genius by Jesus to show the religious hypocrites the reality of their rebellion. Jesus didn't need their stamp of approval. Even though they were the highest religious authority in the land, He didn't need to prove Himself to them. Sometimes our gushing words are a sign of a desperate need to be approved of. Are you like me – the talker? Ever wondered why?

Prayer: Lord, help me to stop and think before I speak, especially when I'm feeling pressurised or vulnerable. Amen.

Hush Hush

BIG PICTURE:
Mark 11:27–33
James 1:19–20

FOCUS:
'… Jesus said, "Neither will I tell you by what authority I am doing these things."'
(Mark 11:33)

… life doesn't need to be about us telling everybody everything …

Session 2:
Nothing but the Truth

When do you do your best thinking?

FOR GROUP DISCUSSION:

• What is your favourite memory verse and why?

• We are horrified when we see Scripture used to justify apartheid, slavery and capital punishment for minor offences. Can you think of modern-day examples of Scripture being used to justify behaviour that you think is wrong or unhelpful?

• If a thorny issue came up while you were reading the Bible, where would you go? To books, a church leader or a trusted friend, or somewhere else?

• Jesus' reminder that we should love the Lord with all our heart, soul, mind and strength suggests that He wants us to be well-rounded worshippers. Does your church have a tendency to stress one area over another? What about you, personally?

- How does giving up things for a period such as Lent help us in our progress towards becoming whole people?

- Which aspects of Christianity are basically pretty simple? Why do we often make Christianity complicated?

- Most of us know that God wants us to be doers of the Word and not hearers only. What are some of the barriers to doing what Scripture tells you to do?

PRAYER:
Lord,
Help me to know the truth –
and not to read what I think
into what You say.
Save me from mere belief:
Help me to live out my faith.
Amen.

The power of truth

BIG PICTURE:
Mark 12:1–12
Psalm 119:105–112

FOCUS:
'Your word is a lamp to
my feet and a light for
my path.'
(Psa. 119:105)

HAVE you ever wondered why it's so important to read Scripture daily? It's easy, living in the 'quickaholic' culture that we do, to sprint into the day without consciously aligning ourselves with God. In the past I rejected the 'quiet time' as being religious and legalistic but I've learned that a life of discipline and reflection is the only way to live beyond survival.

Jesus teaches the parable of the tenants and exposes a harsh reality. He was about to be rejected by Israel; they had a long history of slamming the door in the faces of all the messengers that God sent. And then He poses the tantalising question, 'Haven't you read this scripture?' (Mark 12:10). Perhaps they were ignorant – or perhaps they were trying to ignore the truth.

But then let's turn that around: the fact that Jesus *did* know and understand the scripture enabled Him to see the most troubling week of His life from a divine perspective; all that was unfolding in Jerusalem was more than just hard-hearted behaviour and rejection – something was going on that was 'marvellous in our eyes'. And Jesus recalls the word that the Father had spoken to Him at baptism, as He inserts the tiny – but significant – detail of a beloved son sent (Mark 12:6).

Clothe yourself with what God has said. Don't forget to actually read the scriptures given each day with these daily notes (it's too easy to cheat!). Be equipped by His Word today to face the challenges and opportunities of a new week.

Prayer: Father, help me to read, remember and respond to Your Word, as a vital lamp that lights up my footsteps. Amen.

RECENTLY, as I waited in the baggage claim area at Denver Airport, I found myself pondering the fact that people speak very differently when they are under pressure. We saw last week that tiredness can turn the mildest soul into a volcanic eruption. As I watched the baggage staff at work, it occurred to me how stupid it is to get upset with those people when your luggage goes walkabout. It's not their fault. They didn't lose it. They are trying to help you find it; be nice.

Then my thoughts were interrupted by Kay, who informed me that *our* bags were lost and I'd need to chat with those folks that I had been having such warm thoughts towards moments earlier. I think I did fairly well. As a self-confessed blabber (remember my confession earlier) I want wise, kind words to emerge from my lips when the heat is on. I'd like to be measured and in control when under pressure.

The religious big guns were firing a variety of bullets at Jesus and He was under pressure – they were looking to trap Him – the word here means 'to ensnare a wild animal'. Firstly, they tried to grease the ground beneath Him with their flattery – which didn't affect Him at all. Then came the roundhouse punch, a clever political trap about taxpaying. A wrong word here might put Him at the head of a rebellion (Acts 5:37) or liable to a charge of treason (Luke 23:2). His measured response, brief but loaded with wisdom, was astonishing. May we be like Him. (And my bags showed up the next day.)

Prayer: May I be wise, not to myself but before You. Fill me with Your Spirit; teach me Your ways. Amen.

Wisdom under pressure

BIG PICTURE:
Mark 12:13–27
James 3:13–18

FOCUS:
'Then Jesus said to them, "Give to Caesar what is Caesar's and to God what is God's." And they were amazed at him.'
(Mark 12:17)

... be nice

Loving God

Mark 12:28–30
Deuteronomy 6:1–9

FOCUS:
'Love the Lord your God
with all your heart and
with all your soul and
with all your mind and
with all your strength.'
(Mark 12:30)

BEAR in mind, once more, that Jesus is in His last week on earth. This is a time for last wills and testaments, for parting words and memorable speeches. The three epic years of training the Twelve are ending: a sort of graduation day for them is ahead. And now, a teacher of the law gives Jesus the opportunity to express what the ultimate priority is as he puts the question: which commandment is the most important (Mark 12:28)?

In quoting the Shema (Deut. 6:4–5), the words recited morning and evening by pious Jews, Jesus brings us right back to the heart of everything: loving God. This was what compelled Jesus towards the awfulness and wonder of the cross – His love for the Father motivated Him to set His face like a flint and walk into that storm (John 14:31). Sometimes we focus on the truth that love for *us* took Christ to Calvary, and forget that He went there because of His all-consuming love for God the Father – and His obedience.

When difficulties appear in my life, loving God can slip down my list of priorities. I give my mind to anxiety, my heart to despair and my strength to fixing whatever is wrong – sometimes with little reference to God. Pressure can turn me into one who wants to be the captain of my own soul; I become independent, distanced from God, rather than an eager worshipper. Trouble can turn me into someone with a Christianity that is more of a hobby than the all-embracing, passionate, prioritised loving of God that true discipleship involves. Love God today.

Prayer: Show me how to love You, Lord. Be first, be everything, be my all. Amen.

I ONCE watched a Bible teacher on television whom some describe as 'deep'. I've found out that this can be Christian jargon: sometimes we call a preacher deep when we have absolutely no idea what he or she is talking about.

This chap was putting forward a theory about intercessory prayer that was so complex and muddled that he lost me altogether. Just when I was thinking of turning the television off, he remarked, 'Of course, some of you, who are not spiritually mature, won't be able to understand this teaching.' I punched the 'off' button on my remote control with attitude. Sometimes false teaching slips under the radar because it's disguised as being 'deep' (1 Tim. 1:3–4).

I want to go deeper with God (1 Cor. 2:10; 1 Tim. 3:9) and genuinely fear slipping into a superficial, uninformed faith. But I'm nervous of an excessive complicating of the gospel. The message of Christ is for the child as well as the scholar. When I'm walking through one of 'those weeks', I often find myself coming right back to basics. There is a God. He loves me. My life is in His hands.

The religious leaders of Jesus' day had created a religious maze. Distilling the 613 precepts of the Law down into 365 prohibitions and 248 commands, and wrapping it all up in a tangle of additional man-made legislation, they hijacked holiness. There was even a regulation banning spitting on the sand on the Sabbath (you might inadvertently 'plough a furrow') – which was treated with the same importance as 'Love your neighbour'. Let's keep it simple.

Prayer: Lord, give me depth and maturity, but save me from the lure of complexity and 'revelation' that is disguised error. Amen.

Keep it simple

BIG PICTURE:
Mark 12:31–33
1 Timothy 1:1–7

FOCUS:
'The second is this: "Love your neighbour as yourself." There is no commandment greater than these.'
(Mark 12:31)

The message of Christ is for the child as well as the scholar

17

Intelligent faith

BIG PICTURE:
Mark 12:34–44
1 Thessalonians
5:19–24

FOCUS:
'When Jesus saw that he
had answered wisely ...'
(Mark 12:34)

SOME verses seem to stand out on the page and this one stands out for me. Jesus is appealing for us to have a 'thoughtful faith'. He often posed intricate theological questions to reveal truth to those who would wrestle with the problems He posed. His teaching style makes it clear: we need a thoughtful faith.

Once, I heard a preacher who thoroughly irritated his congregation with an annoying habit: after just about every statement he made, he would pause for dramatic effect and say 'Think about it'. His Sunday morning message must have been punctuated by a hundred 'Think about its'. By the end of the sermon, we were all thinking about what we'd like to do to him.

But although his repetitive exhortation was jarring, his encouragement was correct: we do need to think about our faith, and, as we saw previously, love God with our minds (Mark 12:30).

Paul encouraged the believers in Thessalonica to examine all things critically and keep firm possession of that which was genuine (one commentator's paraphrase of 1 Thessalonians 5:21). The Greek word translated 'critically examine' is the word which describes how a metalsmith scrutinises precious metals to make sure they are genuine. So make sure that you occasionally read a Christian book that stretches your mind and doesn't just entertain you. Ask questions and be willing to wrestle with awkward issues. And consider: do you have a tendency to swallow any teaching that comes along, accepting as gold something that might be brass?

Faith built on clichés and slogans won't work when the storms gather.

Prayer: Father, error comes well disguised. Help me to see through its garb and know truth. Amen.

'Think about it'

Session 3:
Big-Picture Thinking

ICEBREAKER:
Think back to leaving school. If you were listed in a school yearbook as 'Most likely to ...', what might your friends have said of you? (Or what did they say of you?!)

FOR GROUP DISCUSSION
• When you think of the future how do you feel:
  a) fearful; b) buoyant; c) relaxed; d) something else?

• Jesus says that we shouldn't worry about 'tomorrow', implying that we should take each day as it comes. When are you most tempted not to do this? What would you say to someone who is a perpetual worrier?

• Does modern society fool us into believing that we have more control over our life than we actually have?

• Many Christians use the period of Lent to let go of things that hinder and restrict them. What might you be holding onto rather too tightly?

• What mental images help you to imagine the bigness of God?

• How easy do you find it to say: 'I don't know'?
(Think about when you answer your children, respond to non-believing friends questioning you about your faith or meet with acquaintances you don't know well.)

PRAYER:
Father,
Today is Yours,
and tomorrow is already before You.
Grant me hope, courage and faith
for all that is to come.
Amen.

I LOVE the grandeur of the big city, whether it is the sleek, shimmering skyscrapers of San Francisco or the austere old beauty of historic London. But there's something overwhelming, intimidating even, about the city, especially when I think about seeing the gospel making an impact. There are just so many people teeming in the streets. The massive buildings speak of power that will not be moved; a statement that some things might never change, especially for the good. Those edifices were there before I was and will stand strong long after I'm gone. Their thick pillars tell me that I cannot change much in the world. I am an ant on the anthill.

And I'm quite wrong. Everything can change. The Temple was a statement in stone, a monument that spoke of history, tradition and religious power, a symbol of something enduring. Perhaps the disciples, country people from Galilee, felt their own smallness as they gazed at those massive stones (Mark 13:1). Some of those stones survive to this day and they are 20 to 40 feet long, weighing 100 tons. The polished white stones of the Temple took up one-sixth of the entire city of Jerusalem.

But Jesus saw that this edifice would be overturned, turned into rubble. And demolished it was, in AD 70, by the Romans.

The gospel is no small, privatised belief, a collection of notions put together to help sad people feel better. Jesus stands astride time, knew the future to come and is bigger than any pillar, any planet, any power. He formed the mighty mountains (Psa. 65:6). Everything, truly, can change.

Prayer: Enlarge my vision of You, Lord, and fill me not only with faith, but also with hope. Amen.

Everything *can* change

BIG PICTURE:
Mark 13:1–2
Psalm 65

FOCUS:
"'Look, Teacher! What massive stones! What magnificent buildings!'
"Do you see all these great buildings?" replied Jesus. "Not one stone here will be left on another ...'"
(Mark 13:1–2)

Jesus … is bigger than any pillar, any planet, any power

What you can control

BIG PICTURE:
Mark 13:3–10
John 14:1–4

FOCUS:
'You must be on
your guard. You will
be handed over ...
and flogged in the
synagogues. On account
of me you will stand
before governors and
kings as witnesses ...'
(Mark 13:9)

'IT'S completely out of our control,' our pilot said just now. You guessed it; I'm on yet another plane flight as I write. I'm tapping away at my laptop computer while sitting on the runway on Denver Airport, en route to Chicago and then on to London. Unfortunately, the weather patterns in the Midwest mean that we have been parked here for a couple of frustrating hours and there's no sign of 'wheels up' ahead. Most of the passengers are frustrated (I, of course, am a paragon of peacefulness!). But the pilot is right: this is completely out of everybody's control; nothing can be done. I'll just sit here, and chat with you ...

Sometimes the circumstances of life are such that we have no control over them whatsoever; the cancer strikes; the drunk driver destroys; the earth shudders and the giant wave hits; the big earthquake shakes. So it is for the Christian; Jesus speaks of a time of trouble when those who follow Him will feel like pawns in the cruel hands of persecuting authorities. His turn of phrase, 'You will be handed over', speaks of a season when followers of His would feel totally powerless, as they are shunted around like packages. It would all be completely out of their control.

But although we are at times unable to change our circumstances, we can exercise authority over our reactions to them, as we refuse to allow the wet blanket of discouragement and despair to be draped over us. Elsewhere Jesus commands us not to allow our hearts to be troubled (John 14:1–4) – presumably because we have the ability to control our responses.

Prayer: Lord, help me when I feel helpless. Amen.

FEAR has a fantastic imagination. I am really gifted at dreaming up 'What if?' scenarios, usually involving disaster. As a new Christian, I had a whole set of 'What ifs?' that centred on being persecuted as a Christian. Many of our brothers and sisters around the world *are* persecuted for their faith; in fact more Christians are being martyred now than at any other point in history. So *what if* Britain evolved into a state where Christianity was illegal, and I was thrown into prison, tortured and abused, and my family and I had our lives threatened unless we recanted our faith? How would I do under those harrowing circumstances? *What if?*

How about you? Do you sometimes imagine yourself in traumatic circumstances, and worry about how you'd cope? Just this morning I heard of the tears of a dear couple in our church; yesterday they watched their only son die: he had been a picture of health before he was snatched away without warning. And as I pray for them, the faces of my own children form in my mind. *What if?*

Jesus tells us not to worry about the 'What ifs?' If we're placed before a persecuting court, the Holy Spirit will be in the dock with us, and will help us with words to say (13:11). Life will bring some clouds: no one gets through it without some turbulence. But I don't have the grace for tomorrow's hurricanes, only today's mild storm. Take it one day at a time.

Prayer: Lord, help me to leave tomorrow in Your hands, as I live this day today. Amen.

What if?

BIG PICTURE:
Mark 13:11–12
Matthew 6:25–34

FOCUS:
'Whenever you are … brought to trial, do not worry beforehand about what to say. Just say whatever is given you at the time, for it is not you speaking, but the Holy Spirit.' (Mark 13:11)

Take it one

day at a time

God is still God

BIG PICTURE:
Mark 13:13–23
Acts 4:23–31

FOCUS:
'If the Lord had not cut short those days, no-one would survive. But for the sake of the elect, whom he has chosen, he has shortened them.'
(Mark 13:20)

NO ONE wants to believe in a world governed by nothing. That's why often even the most faithless will 'thank their lucky stars', welcome the black cat that crosses their path, and stroke the rabbit's foot for good luck. When we're being asked to sing in the rain, a debilitating sense of powerlessness can overwhelm us. Prayer can seem pointless, because life seems out of control, a runaway train without brakes, with no one in the driving-seat. Or so it seems. When the rain comes in our lives, the sound of the downpour seems to drown out God's voice and ours too; can He hear us? Why can't we hear Him? Is He ignoring us, making our misery worse? We feel more like victims than victors, buffeted by the winds of chance, with no higher authority that is interested or powerful enough to intervene. God seems to be smaller than the tumour, overshadowed by the overdraft, intimidated by the redundancy letter. Much more of this and He will disappear forever.

But amid all the promised pain that Jesus prophesies, both around the fall of the Temple in Jerusalem in AD 70 and also during the end times, still we see the sovereign hand of God, overriding it all with His utter authority, placing limits on the level of suffering. Fresh from arrest and threats, Peter, John and their friends celebrate their 'sovereign Lord' (Acts 4:24). Of course, we'd all prefer suffering and evil to be totally banished, as one day it will be. In the meantime, we live in a hard, painful world – but not one that God has deserted.

Prayer: Help me to know that, even in the darkest times, You will never leave me. Amen.

ONE morning recently, my mobile phone beeped in the early hours with a text message from a friend, who is battling a tsunami wall of problems. She is clinging to God, but unable to think much, or pray with any energy. I sent a text back which included a simple statement: God is bigger.

We saw yesterday that troubled times can shrink our vision of God. The things that intimidate and overwhelm us can appear to tower over God – He's not big enough to cope. But as Jesus continues to talk about the turbulence of the end times, He reminds us that He is bigger than the biggest things we can contemplate.

The sun, moon and stars were symbols of power in the ancient world; yet here, using poetic language, the light of that blazing orb called the sun turns to shade; moonlight becomes a memory and even the stars take a dive from their solid positions in the sky. This is symbolic language and so we are not always to take it literally (Peter in Acts 2:15–21 applies the prophecy of Joel about the sun and moon to the events on the day of Pentecost). But the real point is that the Son of Man is painted as the One who comes surfing on the clouds, 'with great power and glory', bigger, stronger, greater than them all, far above 'all rule and authority, power and dominion, and every title that can be given, not only in the present age but also in the one to come' (Eph. 1:21). Ask God to renew your vision of Him. It's probably been shrunk by life.

Prayer: With Moses, Lord, I pray, 'Show me Your glory.' Amen.

The power and the glory

BIG PICTURE:
Mark 13:24–37
Ephesians 1:15–23

FOCUS:
'At that time men will see the Son of Man coming in clouds with great power and glory.'
(Mark 13:26)

God is bigger

Session 4:
Moments of Truth

ICEBREAKER:

In the film, *The Bucket List*, two terminally ill men escape from a cancer ward and head off on a road trip with a wish list of 'things to do' before they die. What would be on your list?

FOR GROUP DISCUSSION

• People who suffer and believe that God is good are faced with the question: 'So why doesn't God intervene to stop it?' What answer would you give?

• Think for a moment of your closest friends. Do you find it easy to confide in them when things are tough?

• Why might we not 'tell the truth' to God in our personal prayers?

- It is said that Christian growth truly takes place in community. Do you agree?

- Peter's worst day (his denial of Christ) turned out to be his best day (the atonement of his sins). Can you think of bad days in your life that, on reflection, turned out to be good?

- We have all let Jesus down in one way or another. Can you share from your own experience an occasion (from which you learnt) that enabled you to grow stronger as a result?

PRAYER:
Lord,
Help me to be truthful:
in prayer, in friendship,
in times of success and failure.
Amen.

Suffering but still loved

BIG PICTURE:
Mark 14:1–26
Psalm 118:1–14

FOCUS:
'I will not drink again of the fruit of the vine until ... I drink it ... in the kingdom of God.'
(Mark 14:25)

HOW would you spend your last night? I've wondered what my priorities would be if I found myself just a few hours away from an appointment with the executioner. Many Christians around the world face that reality: never forget that tens of thousands are martyred every year because of their love for Jesus Christ. So what if they came for us?

Jesus chose to spend His final hours over a meal with His best friends. The conversation over the food was real, gritty and even awkward, with moments of tension and sadness. And there was time to remember what was important, with bread broken and wine sipped.

Then a song was sung; music carries a power to move and strengthen us, to unite and to solidify truths that life has eroded. The hymn chosen would have been the *Hallel*, part of Psalms 115–118. So what words did Jesus use on His last night? We'll pause for a couple of days and consider His worship.

He proclaimed that God is good and that His love is eternally enduring (Psa. 118:1–5). Suffering can whisper a dark accusation about God's character – does He really care? Is He bothered about us? Difficult times carry a double power: not only do we suffer but we wonder. Perhaps we battle sickness but then hurt spiritually as well as physically, tormented by thoughts that God is dead or, worse, alive but uncaring.

Jesus embraced suffering convinced that He was loved by His Father – it was the closing stanza of the hymn, the last words He sang (Psa. 118:29). Whatever else you don't know, know this: God loves you.

Prayer: Help me to know Your love for me, Lord, when my circumstances and feelings suggest that I am unloved. Amen.

'I DON'T trust anybody – that way I won't be disappointed.'

So says a friend of mine, who embraces an approach to relationships that I could never share. It's not that he's wrong but that it just wouldn't work for me. As an idealist, I am hopeful, always preferring the happy-ever-after endings, and tending to expect that my friends will be marathoners, partners with me for the distance that is life.

That means that I have had plenty of relational disappointments along the way – and I'm sure that I've not always been all I could have been to my friends. So while I could never adopt my friend's stoic philosophy, I do think that we should approach our relationships with a bit more gritty reality, and shed some of our naivety. We are fallen human beings, saved but still in the process of growth and change.

Jesus was under no illusions about the frailties of those closest to Him; knowing that they depended so much upon His leadership, He realised they would be like lost, lonely sheep on a bleak hillside once He had gone.

And He wasn't swayed by speeches that would ultimately turn out to be hollow aspirations and unfulfilled promises, like Peter's insistence that he would uniquely stay true, prompting a flood of pledges of allegiance from the others that wouldn't survive even one day. Their heady vows would disappear in the dust they made as they fled.

Don't be tormented when those you expect much of disappoint you. They – and we – still haven't graduated from the human condition.

Prayer: Lord, help me hope, without naivety: when I am disappointed, help me to yet hope again. Amen.

Realistic expectations

BIG PICTURE:
Mark 14:27–31
Job 6:14–20

FOCUS:
""You will all fall away,"
Jesus told them, "for it is
written: 'I will strike the
shepherd, and the sheep
will be scattered.'"
(Mark 14:27)

Don't be tormented when those you expect much of disappoint you

The stunning surprise of trouble

BIG PICTURE:
Mark 14:32–34
Hebrews 5:7–8

FOCUS:
'He took Peter, James and John along with him, and he began to be deeply distressed and troubled.' (Mark 14:33)

PAUSE and take a long look at this remarkable scene, as we see Jesus struggling; He is 'deeply distressed and troubled' – the words include a sense of amazement, in the same way that the disciples were astonished (Mark 10:32). Jesus knew well enough that death was coming, and had repeatedly tried to explain to His slow-witted disciples what was to come, but then when He finally came face to face with His painful destiny, He naturally recoiled at the awfulness to come. Even though He knew what He knew, He found Himself overwhelmed by horrified surprise. It's one thing to contemplate suffering in the future; it's quite another to find that today is the day of pain.

There's usually an element of surprise in suffering – especially because most of us have little prophetic warning of trouble ahead. Most of us live in the delusion that bad things happen to other people. No one assumes cancer, premature bereavement, or some other tragedy will be part of our life, and so when they are, we go into shock.

But Jesus is open in His struggle and makes no attempt to hide His anguish from His trusted friends. There's no 'stiff upper lip' here, no stoic attitude that pretends all is well. Jesus was in the deepest despair. Faith doesn't smile a grin of fixed pretence: it faces the unfortunate surprises of life with reality. If you are facing suffering today, reach out for help. And if those around you are struggling – reach out to them. You can at least make sure that whatever they are going through, they don't go through it alone.

Prayer: Lord, help me weep without shame with others when I need to; to know their strong support when life slides downhill. Amen.

JESUS did not want to go to the cross. He would have been very familiar with this cruel and agonising method of execution used by the Romans and quite naturally recoiled from the pain to come. Understandably, He pleads with the Father, hopeful that there might be some other way. There's tender intimacy here as He addresses the Father using the Aramaic word 'Abba' – this was later used by the Early Church (Rom. 8:15). 'Abba' is the name which every Jewish child still uses within the home to address their father. It's a tender term that speaks of intimacy and trust.

Jesus spends three specific periods crying out to God but punctuated His prayer times by going back to His disciples. Sadly, they were exhausted and were deep in sleep even while He battled.

But notice that Jesus leaned on *two* resources in this His darkest hour – prayer to His Father, and companionship with His friends. He breaks His times of intense intercession twice to go back and be with them. God comforts us – and often uses human beings as the agents of that comfort (2 Cor. 7:6).

When I'm stranded in one of life's downpours, I need to talk to God and talk with my friends. We need prayer and people both.

Prayer: Lord, thank You for the people you place around me. Remind me to talk with my friends as well as with You when I need help. Amen.

Prayer and people

BIG PICTURE:
Mark 14:35–65
2 Corinthians 1:3–7

FOCUS:
'Then he returned to his disciples and found them sleeping.'
(Mark 14:37)

We need prayer and people both

SESSION 4: DAY 5

Why deny?

BIG PICTURE:
Mark 14:66–72
Isaiah 40:29–31

FOCUS:
'He began to call down curses on himself, and he swore to them, "I don't know this man you're talking about."'
(Mark 14:71)

THIS tragic episode describes the lowest point of Peter's life, as he infamously denies Jesus, exactly as prophesied, in synch with a nearby crowing rooster even. But just why did he cave in as he did? He was so totally convinced that he would pass the test and stand unwaveringly as a follower of Jesus: now he explodes with rage and calls down curses upon himself, so desperately does he want to distance himself from the newly-arrested prisoner. What has gone wrong?

In the first place, Peter was exhausted – we know that from the disciples' droopy-eyed performance in Gethsemane. Sleep deprivation is dangerous; good people do bad things when their energy levels are seriously depleted. Secondly, he was probably already seriously disappointed in himself, with all that sword swinging, ear removal, and then the desperate scramble from the garden when Jesus was arrested. When we feel the flush of failure, we can lose hope: the flawed logic is simple: I've already made a mess of things, so what does it matter if I wade further into the mire?

And then probably raw fear was the final straw for Peter. 'Below in the courtyard', implies that Jesus was upstairs when the Sanhedrin met. Perhaps Peter could hear the blood-curdling jeering, and the terrible sound of fists pummelling flesh, as the blindfolded prisoner became a helpless punchbag for soldiers and priests.

Fatigue, failure and fear; this was a lethal cocktail that turned a good man into a cursing coward. Thankfully, forgiveness and restoration were available.

Fatigue, failure and fear … a lethal cocktail …

Prayer: Keep me strong, hopeful, and courageous, Lord. May my life today express loyalty to You, not denial of You. Amen.

Session 5:
Painful Times

ICEBREAKER:
Misunderstandings are the staple diet of soaps and sitcoms. What is your most amusing misunderstanding?

FOR GROUP DISCUSSION

• Self-control is a fruit of the Spirit, so should develop as we grow spiritually. But it is also an area of our lives we can cultivate. If you could know instant self-control in one area, where would you want it to be? What practical steps might you need to take to be self-controlled in that area?

• When you're accused, are you more likely to say nothing or to fly off the handle? Can you think of times when it's best to keep quiet when accused and times when it's best to say something?

• Most would argue that it is good to have biblical convictions. How can we still be generous to our opponents?

- Whom do you envy? What damage does envying do?

- Have you ever suffered verbal abuse, or something similar, for being a Christian? How did you respond?

- It used to be more popular to 'nail your colours to the mast' (ie tell people that you are a Christian early on in a relationship). Do you agree that Christians are less eager to do so nowadays? Why do you think this is?

PRAYER:
Lord,
Teach me to be faithful,
but not brutal,
as I share my love for You.
Help me to be a person of conviction
without unhelpful confrontation.
Amen.

HAVE you ever found yourself accused, because someone has taken something that you said – perhaps out of context – and then twisted it just enough to indict you? As someone who speaks from a lot of platforms, that happened to me recently. I was incensed, desperate to defend myself and put the record straight. And sometimes it's important to do just that – to clarify a misunderstanding. As we'll see, Jesus epitomises supreme self-control as the religious leaders battered Him with fists and falsehoods – but He did insist on clearing up one important matter.

Those little men with loud voices had reached a decision, and the trial stood at a critical point. As a Jewish council, they had only one capital crime to present to Pilate: treason. The accusation was that Jesus had claimed to be a king and, as a dangerous revolutionary, He was a threat to Roman rule. Six times in this chapter Jesus is called 'the king' (verses 2, 9, 12, 18, 26, 32). The Jewish leaders knew that a religious charge would not make Pilate indict Jesus, so they trumped up a political charge.

Pilate put the question: 'Are you the king of the Jews?'

Mark's account implies that Jesus simply said that He was indeed the King. But then John's Gospel shows us another camera angle, as Jesus explains that He is not claiming kingship in the usual human sense, with an army to resist His arrest, but that His kingdom is 'from another place' (John 18:36). He poses no military threat. Sometimes, it's good to defend ourselves and clarify misunderstandings. But not always, as we'll see tomorrow …

Prayer: Show me when to speak, and when not, Lord. Deliver me from fear of speaking up and from speaking rashly. Amen.

Setting the record straight …

BIG PICTURE:
Mark 15:1–2
John 18:33–38

FOCUS:
'"Are you the king of the Jews?" asked Pilate. "Yes, it is as you say," Jesus replied.' (Mark 15:2)

Sometimes, it's good to defend ourselves and clarify misunderstandings. But not always …

... and staying silent

BIG PICTURE:
Mark 15:3–5
Isaiah 53:1–7

FOCUS:
'But Jesus still made no reply, and Pilate was amazed.' (Mark 15:5)

THE ancient Jewish writer Philo once said that 'Envy naturally attaches itself to whatever is great.' No wonder the magnificent Jesus provoked envy in the sad men who accused Him (Mark 15:10). Envy is a toxic force, the root cause of all kinds of trouble. Scripture warns us that, 'where you have envy and selfish ambition, there you find disorder and every evil practice' (James 3:16). Like a corrosive acid, envy will eat a hole in our souls. The religious hierarchy, driven to distraction with jealousy, get their fangs into Jesus and the venom of multiple accusations pours out. It's a scene of sheer evil. Matthew Henry astutely remarks that corrupt priests are generally the worst of men. Be wary of some religious, Bible-toting zealots. Driven to do terrible things in the name of God, they are the not-too-distant cousins of those who burned people at the stake in the name of Jesus.

But if the wrath of the priests is shocking, then the silence of Jesus in the face of their insults and false charges is all the more remarkable, as Pilate noticed with some amazement. He steadfastly refused to respond to their baiting. Silence in a Roman law court did not imply guilt.

We need to ask God for wisdom to know when to defend ourselves, but also to know when silence is golden. Certainly there are some occasions when even a million words would never satisfy our critics: perhaps at times like that, we're better to leave our case with the God who is able to vindicate those who truly are innocent.

Prayer: Give me wisdom, grace, and self-control when I am criticised unfairly, Lord. Amen.

RECENTLY I was in Ethiopia, visiting some amazing initiatives to care for children who are in a truly desperate situation. I expected to be shocked and moved by the raw, crushing poverty, and I was. I braced myself for the harrowing experience of sitting at the bedside of a woman who was about to succumb to the ravages of AIDS. But I was moved more by the sheer beauty and selflessness of these most stunning people. I have never bumped into such unashamed love or sacrificial welcome, or witnessed community as I have seen it in that visit, where neighbours rush to adopt AIDS orphans (despite their own desperately stretched resources), not even because they have faith but because they simply see it as the right thing do. I was told the cities were generally safe places day and night and that the crime rate is low, which amazed me. If I had nothing, what measures might I take to feed my own children? Selflessness is always an arresting, breathtaking sight, one to behold and treasure.

As Jesus hung on the cross, the repeated cry from the crowd summed up their expectation of what a man in dire straits would do: save himself. But the cross stands as an eternal reminder that there is another way, a way that will always attract attention in a grabbing, greedy world. It's where we live and die to give, rather than to take; to serve, rather than be served. Want to pull a crowd? Live like a servant.

Prayer: Help me put self second today God, and grant me opportunities to serve. Amen.

Selflessness and selfishness

BIG PICTURE:
Mark 15:6–32
Matthew 20:26–28

FOCUS:
'Those who passed by hurled insults at him, ... saying, "So! You who are going to destroy the temple and build it in three days, come down from the cross and save yourself!"'
(Mark 15:29–30)

Selflessness is always an arresting, breathtaking sight, one to behold and treasure

Utterly alone

BIG PICTURE:
Mark 15:33–41
Psalm 22

FOCUS:
'And at the ninth hour
Jesus cried out in a loud
voice, "*Eloi, Eloi, lama
sabachthani?*"– which
means, "My God, my
God, why have you
forsaken me?"'
(Mark 15:34)

MARK doesn't give us a detailed, blow by blow description of the bloody horrors of death by crucifixion: he succinctly affirms, 'And they crucified him', sparing us the gory details (Mark 15:24). The fact is that there was something far more awful than even the most gouging wounds from those cruel whips or the shocking piercing of the nails; that was the sense of abandonment and aloneness that Jesus felt as He took upon Himself the megaton weight of the sins of the world. As we consider Him hanging there, we peer into a mystery, as He plunged into a black hole of being utterly, totally cut off. To be alone in the universe, the pawn of chance or luck, with no God available to help or thank, is no life at all. A poet once spoke with pride at the thought of being the captain of his own soul. I can't think of anything worse; life without God is desolate and meaningless.

Yet today there are still so many who are hauling themselves through life, scrabbling to heal their own wounds, be the answer to their own prayers, and survive as models of self-sufficiency. God, as far as they are concerned, is either non-existent or indifferent.

Jesus tasted that sense of desolation and separation from the Father, so that we might be reunited and partnered with God forever. Are you watching someone you love who is singing in the rain? Pray for strength, for wisdom, for endurance, but most important of all, pray that they may know God Himself, up close and personal.

**Prayer: For those who do not know You, let me be a
light, a servant, a life that points to You. Amen.**

LIFE is full of unexpected heroes. I have been praying for my friend, Canon Andrew White. You could pass him in the street and never be aware of the brave heart that is his. I've been with Andrew and watched him at work in the Israeli/Palestinian conflict in Jerusalem. As I write this, he is away from his family home yet again, desperately trying to help bring some calm to the continual chaos in Baghdad. And, as well as all this, Andrew battles huge health problems every day. But massive challenges often serve as the stage upon which unlikely heroes tread.

So it was with Joseph of Arimathea. While the disciples of Jesus were in hiding, it was this good man who attended to the dead body. He was prominent, rich and a disciple of Jesus (Matthew 27:57) but had been a secret, underground follower because of fear (John 19:38). But now he nails his colours to the mast and, literally in Mark's version, 'becomes bold', goes to Pilate and asks for the body of Jesus. John tells us that Joseph was joined by Nicodemus, who had previously quietly visited Jesus at night time (John 3): now he too openly declares himself as a friend and follower of Christ (John 19:39). Sometimes extreme pressure nudges us to discover strength that we hardly knew we had.

Perhaps you're facing some massive turbulence today. Is it possible that God is inviting you to step into a new phase of courageous faith? Perhaps an unexpected silver lining in your cloud is the discovery of strength that you never felt was in you.

Prayer: Let me be a hero in the ordinary today. Take me to a new level of faith, love and service. Amen.

Unexpected heroism

BIG PICTURE:
Mark 15:42–47
John 19:38–42

FOCUS:
'Joseph of Arimathea, a prominent member of the Council, who was himself waiting for the kingdom of God, went boldly to Pilate and asked for Jesus' body.'
(Mark 15:43)

Sometimes extreme pressure nudges us to discover strength that we hardly knew we had

Session 6:
Risen Indeed

ICEBREAKER:
How are you with dates? Have you ever forgotten an important date (birthday, wedding anniversary, interview)?

FOR GROUP DISCUSSION
- Most Christians know that 'Christ is risen'. How can we make this reality a part of our daily lives?

- Think ahead to the next few weeks. How might the reality of the 'risen Christ' change your perspective?

- The end of Mark's Gospel includes some unusual miracles. Have you ever viewed or experienced 'a miracle'? How did you respond?

- Can you think back to a teaching series, a course or a series of videos/DVDs that made an impact on your life?

- Deep down, most Christians know the areas in which their faith needs to grow. Which area would you ask for prayer for, if someone were praying for you?

PRAYER:
Lord,
You are risen and ascended today.
May I live in Your power, Your victory and Your love.
Amen.

Forgetting the resurrection

BIG PICTURE:
Mark 16:1–8
1 Corinthians
15:12–34

FOCUS:
'Very early ... just after sunrise, they were on their way to the tomb and they asked each other, "Who will roll the stone away from the entrance of the tomb?"'
(Mark 16:2–3)

IT SEEMS somewhat bald to put it this way, but here goes: I keep forgetting the resurrection. In the blur of everyday life and ministry, the incredible truth that Jesus is very much alive, right now, can get buried, filed away as a mere theological belief, part of a creed that I say, a conviction that I carry, but little more. I talk about Jesus every day of my life, but sometimes the avalanche of words sweeps away the core truth: He is risen.

The two Marys and Salome, hurrying to the tomb of Jesus, are certainly to be admired for their devotion. Sadly, they had missed the point about the resurrection too. Even though Jesus had repeatedly said that He would rise on the third day, the truth had not quite landed with them (Mark 9:9–10,31; 10:34).

When you forget the resurrection, you waste a lot of life on things that don't matter – like carrying spices to anoint a body that isn't there. You fret, anxious about apparently insurmountable problems when, actually, these things have been taken care of. Because Jesus is alive, even the biggest stones can become parking spots for passing angels (Matt. 28:2). When you forget the resurrection, you weep rather than witness. Faith is useless and forgiveness a vain hope (1 Cor. 15:14,17).

Of course, it takes practice to accept the really good news. Initially the poor women were terrified into silence. But eventually, thankfully, they got it. He really has risen. Got that?

Prayer: I affirm my faith in You, now, Lord Jesus, the resurrection and the life, my coming King. Amen.

THERE'S a lot of debate among scholars about the authenticity of these verses in Mark – some manuscripts don't include them. But let's still consider them – they are a valuable summary of the beliefs of the Early Church and don't contradict other scripture.

Jesus' appearance to Mary Magdalene is wonderful, especially in a culture where women were denigrated. Jesus sweeps away the prejudices by making Himself known to a woman – and one with such a dark past.

But in his Gospel, John paints a more tender portrait of their meeting. Mary's eyes were swollen with tears of despair but then He appears: not in a blinding flash of light, or with a drum roll or fanfare but as someone that you could mistake for the gardener. It's only when He speaks her name that she suddenly realises the truth. It's Jesus!

There were so many things He could have said at that moment. 'I told you so.' 'Death is finished!' 'Mission accomplished.' 'I've got the keys of death and hell.' But instead, Jesus' priority was to reassure one of His distressed followers.

When it comes to friendship, Jesus really does know how to do it. Let's ask Him to bless our friendships, to help us when they are under threat and to teach us how to be the kind of friends that others treasure.

Prayer: Lord Jesus, thank You for showing me how to be a true friend. Help me to be like You in my friendships. Amen.

One word

BIG PICTURE:
Mark 16:9–13
John 20:11–20

FOCUS:
'When Jesus rose early
on the first day of the
week, he appeared first
to Mary Magdalene …'
(Mark 16:9)

When it comes to
friendship, Jesus
really does know
how to do it

43

SESSION 6: DAY 3

Charming snakes

BIG PICTURE:
**Mark 16:14–18
Acts 28:1–6**

FOCUS:
'In my name they will drive out demons; ... they will pick up snakes with their hands; and when they drink deadly poison, it will not hurt them at all ...'
(Mark 16:17–18)

IN AMERICA, there are some churches (thankfully only a few) that take these verses so literally that they dance with snakes and drink poison as part of their services. Viewing their worship on television is a disturbing experience, as they work themselves into an ecstatic frenzy, and then pass the reptiles around. All of this is supposed to demonstrate faith. Most of the congregation have been bitten, and some have died. Deliberately dicing with venom and poison is not what is being suggested here. Jesus *did* say that we had power over snakes (Luke 10:19) and Paul did escape an encounter with a viper unharmed, but he was building a fire at the time, not deliberately reaching into a basket (Acts 28:3).

And we've already noted that this text is unreliable: I'd like something a little more solid before waltzing with a rattlesnake or taking a sip of cyanide. One commentator notes that a better translation would be 'if they are *compelled* to take up snakes or drink poison' (by a persecutor). These sincere but seriously misled people who provoke serpents are doing little more than tempting God (Matt. 4:5–7) as they deliberately expose themselves to danger.

But some of us do that in more subtle ways. Some in the Early Church specifically sought martyrdom, believing it to be the most glorious death. They brought trouble upon their own heads. Sometimes in our misplaced zeal, our thoughtless words, our clumsy attempts to stand for Christ, we stir up trouble unnecessarily. It's important to be bold enough to suffer for *doing good* (1 Pet. 3:17); it's madness to suffer for being foolish. Trouble will come, that's a promise. But don't go hunting for it.

Prayer: Lord, increase my faith, and save me from fanaticism. Amen.

WE PRAYED yesterday and asked the Lord to increase our faith – which is no mean feat. It's a fact that's often overlooked but Jesus spent six weeks after His resurrection when He constantly appeared to His disciples and spoke about the kingdom of God (Acts 1:3), with disciples who seemed more interested in discussing the earthly kingdom of Israel (Acts 1:6). Narrow thinking dies hard.

And then Luke makes it clear that He gave 'many convincing proofs to them' that He really was alive. I'm encouraged that Jesus worked so hard to build their faith before finally ascending to be with His Father.

Sometimes I feel so very guilty about my lack of faith: over the years I've seen far more than my fair share of God's activity and supernatural power, so much so that I often feel that He 'spoils' me – and yet I still possess an uncanny ability to worry – and wonder. But I find myself in good company; one might have thought that a couple of hours, or even a day or two, in the private company of the resurrected Jesus would be enough to galvanise the disciples' faith and strengthen them for the challenges ahead – but it took a further crash course that lasted a whole six weeks!

Sometimes we can be tempted to promote the incredible little band that was Jesus' disciples into super-sainthood, but the fact is that they were just like us, with our capacities for greatness and grime, for passion and passivity, and for faith as well as unbelief. He worked with them. He'll work with us too.

Prayer: Train me to believe, Lord. And thank You for enrolling me in the lifelong academy of faith. Amen.

Six incredible weeks

BIG PICTURE:
Mark 16:19
Acts 1:1–11

FOCUS:
'After the Lord Jesus had spoken to them, he was taken up into heaven …'
(Mark 16:19)

He worked with them. He'll work with us too

Just as He said

BIG PICTURE:
Mark 16:19–20
Hebrews 1

FOCUS:
' ... and he sat at the right
hand of God.'
(Mark 16:19)

SO THE epic story draws to an end. It's usually here, if I read a book or watch a movie, that I feel a sense of elation (if the ending has been a happy one) followed quickly by a sense of dissatisfaction, as I remember that even the best story is just that – a story. The lights in the cinema come up and reality lands upon me with a crash: my time of escapism has finished.

But this is not so with the story of Jesus. So utterly changed were His disciples, they embark on a life-and-death mission in partnership with the Lord who works with and through them, casting all cares for their own survival aside as they throw themselves into the mission and march, heads down against the torrent of rain that is persecution, to turn the world the right way up.

And all that Jesus said and sang about His own future came true. At that final meal, we remember that He sang about the right hand of God. When He stood before His accusers, He affirmed that the right hand of God was where He was heading. And now, we see that all of this was not bluster or rhetoric but, His work finished yet ever-continuing through His people, He ascends and sits triumphant at that very place.

Sometimes, when the weather of life is at its worst, and we wonder if we'll ever see the sunshine again, it's good to remember: He is safely home. And one day, we will be home safe too.

He is safely

home

Prayer: Continue Your mission, in and through me, all the days of my life, until I see You face to face, risen Lord Jesus. Amen.

Be inspired and challenged by Jeff Lucas' Life Journeys DVDs

Thought-provoking resources for individual and small-group use

Learn from Jeff Lucas' perceptive wisdom as he gently and humourously corrects common misconceptions and makes Scripture relevant with his practical insights.

Elijah – Prophet at a Loss
Take courage from the challenges Elijah faced in his walk with God.
EAN: 5027957001107

Friends Rediscovered
Take a practical, in-depth look at friendship through the life of the apostle Paul.
EAN: 5027957001091

Stop Looking for the Will of God
Discover God's plan for your life by seeking Him first.
EAN: 5027957000957

A Walk on the Wild Side
Learn lessons in faith from the life of Jonah.
EAN: 5027957000964

Only £18.99 each (DVD pack includes a personal booklet)
Extra personal booklets available: £2.50 each

'My Bible study group has so enjoyed the series by Jeff Lucas. His relaxed manner and wonderful insights have helped us to grow.'

Prices correct at time of printing